False Tongues of Fire

A Personal Testimony

By
Betty Jewell

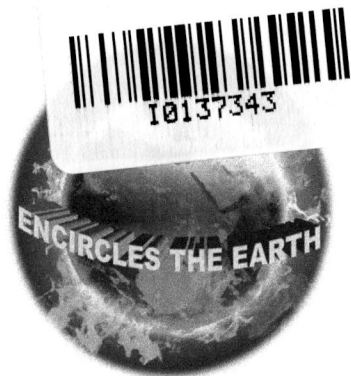

———————————————

Copyright © 2013 Aspect Books
ISBN-13: 978-1-4796-0226-1 (Paperback)
ISBN-13: 978-1-4796-0227-8 (epub)
ISBN-13: 978-1-4796-0228-5 (Kindle/Mobi)
Library of Congress Control Number: 2013911349

Published by
AB **ASPECT Books**
www.ASPECTBooks.com

Haunted by Fear

God was good to me in the testimony I give, for the
Spirit of Fear
Haunted my life, for a period of three years.
No One can know except the Lord, the misery of
my soul
But thanks to God His power and might my story
can be told.

No one escapes the pattern of sin, stalking and
spreading like disease from within.
When we think to do good, and with effort we try
We forget the first rule, "to sin we must die."
And … as the story unfolds …

Slowly, but surely, lustful passion captured my soul!
I wept and cried and often I tried to gain a victory
    here.
Those devils that captured the Demoniacs at will,
Camped at my door, possessing me through and
    through.

For many days, weeks, months, and years I prayed,
    resisting my foe,
I fought against powers that set traps for me, to con-
    quer, as they set their goals.
Night after night as I lay in the dark, tormented and
    troubled, my mind in great fear,
Many voices I heard spoke right in my ears, I tossed
    and turned almost three years.

Those devils set up housekeeping in me, and dared
    that I pray, to be released!!
Oh God! What could I do? Nothing, but pray the
    whole year through.
Tortured by fear and ruled from within, death would
    be welcome, that's what they knew!!
I realized I was loosing my mind and cried, "Oh
    God! Help me! I need you!"

Commencing in prayer wasn't easy to do, as fear
    gripped me, and chained me like a prisoner,
Sore afraid and not able to see, those unseen devils
    that leered at me.
But like the Demoniacs of old, the word of God and
    the love of Jesus, made me whole.

Chapter One

According to God's Word, when ever we pray, the Holy Spirit, with groanings and utterings interprets our prayer requests to a pure, perfect Holy God. The Holy Spirit, with unerring accuracy, knows exactly the mind of the soul's request and can speak in heavenly language.

Jesus left us an example of His prayer life, instructing that his disciples address, "His Father" as "Our Father" which art in heaven." The disciples had spent three and a half years with Jesus and knew his habits, especially that of his prayer life. Often He would rise early before daybreak and seek His Father alone, quiet, without any interruptions. To seek His Father in prayer was His greatest joy, for He had come from Heaven and knew His Father, personally. Knowing his own father intimately, it wasn't necessary for Him to speak in an "unknown tongue." Jesus spoke Hebrew and His Father, the author of all languages, understood.

After His resurrection, Jesus met with his disciples several times, and upon his last meeting He commanded them to remain in Jerusalem and wait for the promise of the Father, saying they will be baptized not with water, but with the Holy Ghost. (Acts 1:4, 5). They waited as commanded. During this period of time, they prayed. All were in one accord, as their minds, souls, and hearts were with the One whom they loved and were knit one with another. Suddenly, as the sound of a mighty rushing wind, the Holy Spirit filled the room, and "tongues of fire" sat upon each of the disciples signifying that the Living God was among them. They were filled with His Holy Spirit, qualifying each to be a mighty witness for Him, and they spoke in "other tongues" as the Spirit gave utterance. It was the yearly Jewish Passover celebrated by Jews having traveled far from their own home lands. They were from many different countries and spoke different languages other than Hebrew. They had traveled great distances to keep this special holy feast, centuries old. The death, burial and resurrection of Jesus Christ had taken place prior to this yearly feast. Must these Jews leave not knowing about the great sacrifice that had taken place, nor learn about the true Messiah and the message of salvation? The prophecies had been fulfilled, Jesus had come, and now everyone should know!

Chapter Two

On the day of Pentecost, the disciples were filled with the Holy Spirit and began to speak in other tongues as the Spirit gave utterance and the visiting Jews heard in their own languages the gospel of Christ. Acts 2: 1-11. They were astonished! These humble fishermen spoke with accuracy, the languages of those present. It was a miracle! There was no language barrier, for God provided a way that His people know about His Son's great sacrifice in their behalf. No reports of disciples fainting, lying on the ground, "slain in the Spirit" jabbering another language not understood by them or anyone. Certainly not an emotional, crying session experience, being exhausted physically. The prophecies had been fulfilled according to the Prophet Joel (Joel 2:28). And the disciples spoke with accuracy, other languages to be understood, promoting the gospel of Christ.

God gives us a mind, and through this created channel, we can reason, think and act. We receive and deposit words, impressions and feelings. In the book of Isaiah 1:18, God says, "Come, let us reason together." One reasons with their intellect, not their feelings. God doesn't ask us to upset our emotions so that our physical being loses its reasoning abilities. God is not the author of confusion. When one is emotionally upset, one does not reason well, nor make wise decisions or good judgements. Our arch enemy, Satan, does not have access to our thoughts. He can only observe our actions and act accordingly, watching for an opportunity to snare us in his net through whatever plan he cunningly devises.

Our Heavenly Father created each one of us and He only, has access to our souls and knows our thoughts (Luke 11:17. Psalms 94:11). He desires we exercise our God-given right to think, choose and act. By Christ's great sacrifice for all mankind is offered freedom. Satan would like to control us, as he does the masses, and he will, if we allow ourselves to tread upon his territory. This is where multitudes are fooled, as he claims the world as his territory.

Not one person can overcome the powers of

evil except through Christ that conquered this foe. Satan sets traps for the individual. He is cunning, deceptive, and plans ahead to spring his traps on the unsuspecting. Prayer, minute prayer for God's protection daily is imperative, especially while in the service of the Lord He would thwart every avenue against the soul's progress to reach out for God if it were not for Jesus. Jesus offers safety and peace against Satan and his host of evil angels. "For we wrestle not against flesh and blood, but against powers and principalities" (Ephesians 6:12)

Abide in Jesus and stay close to Him. He fought against Satan and all his host and won the victory. This victory He gives to you and me. An instant prayer to the Lord squelches the determination of Satan to destroy you or your plans. But be on guard, because the enemy is ever vigilant to trap you.

Chapter Three

I do not believe speaking in tongues today is the sign that one has received God's Spirit that is Holy. Tongues, as Biblically written, are languages to be understood by the receiver in his or her own language, as on the Day of Pentecost, vital to spreading the gospel. Also, if there is one person speaking an "unknown tongue" then let there be an interpreter, that is the case when someone is knowledgeable of language spoken . This is often done at the United Nations. Tongues speaking was a special miracle performed by God to enable his unlearned disciples to speak in languages to spread the message of His son's earthly sacrifice and plan of salvation. Tongues speaking is a gibberish speech spoken by one and making one think they have the unction of the Holy Spirit. Satan is the great deceiver and always counterfeits that which is genuine.

His false tongues of fire has circled the earth and its inhabitants, invading the minds of the Christian world, convincing individuals they have the Spirit of God, when all the time it is that of another Spirit. The tongues movement has swept almost the earth's inhabitants into its ranks, into deceptive thinking. By the great counterfeit manifestation, the world's masses of sincere, dedicated Christian people believe it is a guaranteed sign from heaven they have been filled with the Holy Spirit. The majority of these dear folks love and worship God and truly believe, and they feel right about their experience. Feeling is not enough, because "there is a way that seemth right unto a man,, but the ends thereof the ways of death," Prov 14:12. Also, " to the law and to the testimony, if they speak not according to this word, it is because there is no light in them." Isaiah 8:20, "Narrow is the way that leadeth to eternal life, and few there be that find it" Matt 7:14, and "Broad is the way that leadeth to destruction," Matt 7:13.

Jesus, Our Lord, says, "only those that overcome will have a right to the Tree of Life." Rev 2:7. What does He mean, "overcome?" I've seen supposedly "Holy Spirit" filled Christians with the tongues speaking experience attend theaters of questionable shows, laugh at filthy jokes, and carry on in an un-christlike manner. Many continue to smoke and drink and are still dominated by unhealthy appetites. Yet, there are dedicated, sincere Christians that speak in tongues and follow the teachings of Christ believing that speaking in tongues signifies they are saved. They truely believe it is a gift from God and one must receive this gift, to qualify them to witness. Those who manifests tongue speaking take great pride that they have the true Holy Spirit. They feel others need this, in order to be "filled with the Spirit" and approved of heaven to do God's work.

The entire chapter of John 14, in the New Testament identifies the Holy Spirit. In the beginning of John 14, Jesus gives comfort and assurance to his disciples that they can believe in Him also, as they believe in God He assures them of his relationship with His Father, as well as a home He will be preparing for them. Haven't they traveled with him for three years, leaving their families, houses and occupations? They have faithfully walked and been with Him while on earth. Each one loved Jesus and He knew they did.. He doesn't leave them as orphans and without comfort, but tells them He will send them another Comforter, that he may abide with them for ever, the Spirit of Truth; one that the world cannot see, but they will know him; for he will dwell with them, and be in them. He will send them a person that is an eternal Heavenly Teacher, someone that can guide them, someone that is qualified and from the throne of God, a special unseen ageless majestic person whose identity is one of the members of the triune establishment, God the Father, God the Son, and God the Holy Ghost. God, the Creator of all mankind, assures they will be guided and taught by absolute truth, the pure Word of God. This Holy Ghost cannot be seen, but thru God's own word, He will be in you and keeps company with you as promised by the Living God. He told them to wait for the promise of receiving the Holy Spirit. As he spoke the same assuring words, he was taken up and a cloud received him out of their sight. Acts 1: 8, 9, 10. This promise to His disciples were fulfilled on the Day of Pentecost.

I was also waiting for this promise. I had firmly believed it would happen to me too, according to scripture. I had read in the book of Acts in the Bible that on the Day of Pentecost the disciples were ail together in one place praising an worshipping the Lord putting all their differences behind them. They obeyed the commandment of Jesus to wait As I waited, I was weeping and crying. Hadn't

I been told I should look into my soul and see if I held anything against anyone, asking God's forgiveness and continue praising Him....saying "thank you Jesus, thank you Jesus, Praise the Lord, Praise." This I repeated constantly. I was told by my new-found Christian friends to chant this in order to receive "speaking in tongues," the sign that you have received the Holy Spirit They continued emphasizing the importance of this special gift as given to the early disciples found in the Books of Acts. Is this the way one is suppose to receive God's Holy Spirit and be able to speak to Him in a language only He understands? The sound coming out of the mouths of the mother and daughter with whom I was with began jabbering in a language they said only God could understand. I ask, "Do you know what you are saying?" They said "No." It was a mystery to me to hear another kind of language, yet I heard them many times speak this way while praying. I decided it must be the language of heaven they were talking about. Each time they began in prayer they went into the familiar chant of continual praising and thanking Jesus repeatedly, and the jabbering began. I had attended an Oral Roberts Evangelist meeting in Springfield, Missouri back in the early fifties with these same friends and witnessed others seeking for the same Spirit I went forward to an alter call, then walk to the back entrance the auditorium finding my friends laying on the floor. The two daughters were both speaking tongues while the mother sat next to them on the floor. I thought this very strange, yet several folks were doing the same thing, so I was impressed. I was being convinced this speaking a total different language must be from God.

Carolyn, one of the daughters of this tongue speaking family came for a visit to my house. The hour was late, so I invited her to spend the night as I lived out in the country and could take her back home the next morning. As we were preparing to retire Carolyn ask if I would like to try to receive the Holy Spirit so I could speak in tongues.

My husband was away on a trip, my three small sons were asleep, the house was quiet I considered this a perfect time, rather than wait to attend a church meeting. Carolyn and I knelt, started in prayer, then began the chant We continued for almost an hour. I became very tired resigning myself that seeking to speak in tongues was very difficult to do. About the time I told Carolyn its getting late and I'm growing very weary, suddenly something happened to me. I began to feel my body bearing down as if I were in child labor. I didn't understand what was happening. As it continued I became exhausted from all the muscle strain as if I were giving birth to a baby but without any pain. There came an unfamiliar sound out of my mouth. Carolyn jumped up, shouting my name, and saying, "You've got the Holy Spirit! Your speaking in tongues!" She grabbed my hand and started dancing around in a circle. Despite my exhaustion I joined her, yet all I wanted to do was lay down and go to sleep. I thanked the Lord for giving me His Holy Spirit so I could be a true witness for Him.

The following day, I awoke and started speaking in a strange unknown tongue. I didn't understand what I was saying. The words spoken were entirely a gibberish sound, didn't make sense to me. Upon hearing me speak, Carolyn said, "God really filled you with the Spirit" It was so strange to me, yet I felt God must love me so much that He allowed me to receive the tongues. It made me feel very special, very important"

Chapter Four

Emotionally, I was very vulnerable. My marriage lacked a warmth and love I desperately needed. My husband seldom expressed affection and was out of town weeks at a time with his job. Even when he was home I felt alone. He never entered into any activity towards helping me with the children. There were no family members near, nor my mother around for support The daily care of my children drained me physically and emotionally. But now, knowing that I could speak in tongues, and knowing God loves me, giving me His special gift, I began to look to Him for everything.

After breakfast I told Carolyn I would take her home. I was living on the edge of town in Springfield, and Carolyn's family lived in town. Before leaving,

I received a phone call from a cousin that was passing through town and wanted to see me. We headed for town with the children, stopping to see my cousin, Dub from Texas. Soon as he saw me drive up, he walked over to the car. When he approached I decided I would tell him about my new experience. We greeted one another. So, I started speaking to him in tongues. It shocked him! He stood there without asking one question, finally walking away shaking his head. I never got a chance to explain. I thought to myself, "well he just doesn't understand." He doesn't know how God has given me such a special wonderful gift.

I drove Carolyn to her house, then returned home. The boys were playing as usual in the back seat of the car so they never paid attention to my tongues speaking to my cousin. That entire week was dedicated to my new experience. While the children were outdoors playing I kept busy with household chores. I knew that God was with me every minute. 1 never had to feel alone. One morning while I was brushing my teeth in the bathroom, I was looking in the mirror and suddenly I heard a voice speak to me. It told me to look into my eyes. I automatically obeyed, thinking it must be the Holy Spirit The voice said to me, "You are Jesus." It startled me. I didn't understand the request, for I knew that no man is Jesus. Each time I looked at myself in the mirror the request came again and again. The voice then told me to put on my red jacket and put on my sandals. I obeyed. Once again the voice said, "You are Jesus." This was overwhelming to hear, yet I decided to obey. Hearing and obeying the voice made me feel I truly belonged to God and that the Holy Spirit was with me constantly. I never revealed this to anyone at the time as I held it sacred and besides, like my cousin, no one would understand … only God.

Chapter Five

One evening after the children were asleep I walked over to my neighbors for a brief visit. They were always so loving and kind, always gave me a warm welcome. While visiting, the same voice told me to talk as loud as I can. I didn't question, but obeyed, thinking the neighbor couldn't hear. Shortly after that request, the voice told me to talk very softly. I obeyed. The same command continued for me to talk loud, then soft. I saw a strange look on my neighbor's face, then decided to excuse myself and go home.

During the same week I felt impressed to fast, did not eat any food during the next five days, only drank water, adding a little sugar. I broke my fast on the fifth day as I was beginning to feel weak. During my fast, I cooked regular meals for my children, never putting one morsel in my mouth. Food became very precious, not wasting one scrap of food.

I arranged for a baby sitter the next week so I could go to town and shop. En route, the same voice told me to stop and pick up a hitch hiker on the road. I obeyed. I always obeyed, thinking it was from the Holy Spirit I drove him over to Carolyn's home, but before arriving I told him about Jesus. I was given words to say, and this total stranger accepted the gospel and accepted Jesus as His Saviour. I was convinced that God was using me as His witness. From then on, I relied on the voices to guide me in everything.

My husband returned home after several weeks on his job. He said we needed to move back into town as we lived too far out As usual, he always expected me to make it happen. After he left on his next trip I started house hunting locating a rental on North Fort Street of Springfield. I hired a couple of folks to help in the move, yet I did a lot of packing and moving myself. I carried some very large boxes and baskets that should have been carried by a stronger person yet when I lifted them they felt as light as a feather. This was a mystery to me. Several other mysterious happenings such as pulling large nails out of solid wooden walls without the use of a hammer. During the move I was given different instructions by the voices telling me what to do. I was so certain it was the Holy Spirit that I obeyed. I just knew God was telling me what to do.

After moving and settling into the new place, I started preparing meals for the family as dictated by the voices. These became strange meals … cooking a roast, then basting it with gruitfruit juice. The voice told me this meal was for John, my husband. I didn't question it, I just accepted and complied. The roast turned out very bitter. Meal after meal became anything but tasty. The voices kept commanding me what I should do. I became very tired and weary. I reached exhaustion. I didn't feel like making a bed or washing a dish. The daily care of three lively youngsters was enough in itself. My husband came home after one of his long trips finding we had moved into the new rental. As always, he would lay on the sofa with a magazine or a western pocketbook reading until it was time for a meal. He was completely oblivious to me, except for what he was doing. He never noticed how thin I was, nor how exhausted I was from the move. He never realized my own personal needs. It never occurred to him that I would run out of energy or become tired. He should have been alert to my condition, but wasn't

He never offered to help with the boys when he was home. I felt alone and responsible for the children and their activities. I always felt I was always on duty. I came from a large loving family where everyone helped one another. He had no brothers, only one sister. He never realized my needs, only that I was there to wait on him and take care of the children.

Chapter Six

One Sunday morning as I was telling him something as he was reading, I began to speak in tongues. That got his attention! It just came out I had guarded carefully never to let him hear me do this ... why? The voices warned me against it He stared at me, then as I continued, he slapped me on the face. I began to cry and told him he would lose everyone of his children. I fled from the house, running towards the direction of someone I knew, living three blocks away. I waited inside my friends garage. She finally came. "What are you doing here?" she said. I told her about the incident and she said I was welcome to stay. She was preparing for an evening prayer service that would be held in the garage. The garage was more like an extra enclosed room with a screen door entrance. I waited and soon a few people began coming in. They all began praying and soon were all speaking in tongues. While she was laying her hands on one person I glanced up and saw my husband at the screen door. He saw me, then walked away. In about an hour, one of our friends, Alvin came in and sat down and tried to talk with me. I told him what happened. The voices answered all the questions he ask, also telling him he would experience a heart attack. What came out of my mouth stunned me, but I thought the Holy Spirit was handling the situation. I wouldn't leave with him to go back to my house. After a short time, his wife came to the door, and forced me out of the room, and drove me back to my house. She was a very large, strong woman. Alvin told my husband he needed to show love and concern for me. After they left, I was so tired I went straight to bed. During the night I was given more instructions by the voices, telling me to continually turn to my right side, then to my left. They also told me how wonderful I was, etc. etc. My mind was worn, my body exhausted. I couldn't sleep. I couldn't physically function. The next morning, I told my oldest son to prepare his and the boys own bowl of cereal, either watch tv or go outdoors and play, that mother needed to stay in bed and rest

Without my knowledge, my husband sought help for my condition. He consulted with our Pastor, at the time, also an attorney friend about my condition. He also had my mother come to Springfield from Houston When mother arrived, she was startled by my condition. She couldn't believe I looked so thin and pale having seen me only a year ago on a visit A great fear came upon me that is indescribable. I had my mother hold me close to her numerous times, yet the fear remained. I was so afraid I couldn't function. I thought if she held me close to her body, the fear would go away, but it didn't Yet, having her with me gave me a sense of being loved and cared for despite my fearful condition.

My mind was tired, my body physically worn. The voices were absolutely tormenting me. I never got enough sleep. She took charge of the boys and the house. I'm sure she found the kitchen a real mess from all the crazy meals I had prepared from the condition of my sick mind.

From the moment she came, I told my mother to make the sign of the cross each time she walked through a door in the house. These instructions came from the voices that were real to me. Like my husband, she never knew I was obedient to the voices that dominated my being.

Soon as my mother came, my husband drove me to the hospital accompanied by an attorney friend.

I told them they were taking me to the hospital. They didn't let me know when I got into the car I was being taken to the hospital, but I told them where I was going, and of course the voices let me know. I didn't protest, simply relied on the voices. When we arrived at the Springfield Catholic Hospital I was admitted, and immediately went to a room where they put me to bed. The hour was late when they left. As I lay there, I began to have an anxious feeling why I was there and decided not to stay. I got out of bed, walked down a long hall, found a door marked in red letters with the word, Exit I tried the door but it wouldn't open. Suddenly, I realized I was locked inside. I started walking down other halls looking for a way out One of the nurses found me, took me back to my room putting me to bed. I tried the same thing again. This time I was strapped to the bed. I had lost so much weight I pushed the leather straps over my hips making another attempt to escape. I started down the hall going to different occupied rooms with sleeping patients. This time I was locked inside the room by the same nurse that became angry. I heard the voice tell me to move my bed around and make as much noise as I could. The nurse came back, but this time, she locked me in the room, and gave me a shot with needle.

It was the first sound sleep I had experienced in weeks. When I awoke, I was inside a large bathtub being bathed by an orderly. He told me that I had been given a shock treatment and had been out for three days. I wasn't aware this had happened. I hadn't been told anything by my husband, nor by the voices, I would be given shock treatments. I wasn't aware in my condition what would happen to me and certainly never knew anything about the many treatments to come. As I began to endure the shock treatments I hated my husband blaming him for my condition and everything that happened to me. I felt he really didn't love me. He had left me so many times to care for the children alone and with the entire responsibilities of household duties. My mother was the only family member I wanted to see.

Chapter Seven

Carolyn's father came to the Hospital I was told. He told them there wasn't anything wrong with me because I had received the baptism of the Holy Spirit I learned about his visit after I was released.

I carried my Bible with me all the time, but never read it I had the Holy Spirit and could depend on the voices to guide me.

Voices had me going from room to room asking each patient if they loved the Lord with all their hearts, soul and mind. It was a repeated ritual daily. During breakfast I was ask to say prayers. I shall never forget some of the most beautiful prayers I prayed, as the words were given to me to speak. My eating habits were changing. I didn't want to drink coffee or tea. My mind seem to be clearing and I felt better, yet the voices continued. I was eating well, yet could not sleep. One night as I lay with my Bible by my bedside I heard a voice that sounded different than the others. The voice told me to sleep with my Bible beneath my pillow. I obeyed. The voices stopped. I finally fell asleep. I repeated this each and every night to stop the voices. One of the nurses ask me to type some instructions about knitting. I never made one mistake in my typing. I was also given leather crafts, so I could make belts. I enjoyed working with my hands. Apparently I was making progress because my doctor allowed me to go home to see my children. It was around Christmas time. I had been in the hospital almost three weeks. I was happy and delighted to see my three boys. By this time my mother had returned home, taking my youngest son. My husband's mother had come to take her place to care for the other children.

I had to return to the hospital for a brief time. Finally, I was released to go back home. I was so glad and happy to be walking out of the hospital, when suddenly a voice spoke loud and strong to me. It told me to go and get into a car parked at the curb. The voice was so insistent. I couldn't resist and ran to the car. It was filled with a group of young nurses from the hospital. I suddenly realized what happened, but it was too late. I was whisked back into the hospital for another two weeks stay, plus more shock treatments. They locked me in a room that had no heat and I came down with bad cold. I was sick and my stay in the hospital was extended. When I finally was released again, I stayed home until the doctor advised my husband that I should find a job outside away from the full responsibility of caring for my children. I was under the care of a psychiatrist twice a week. I didn't want to keep going back to see him because all he wanted to do was talk about himself, besides flirt with me, asking what I had under my blouse. He was an older man that held my hand at my request during the shock treatments as I was afraid to take them. I held the doctors hand each time I was given an injection of sodium penethal. I was ask to count to ten each time, but could count only to three, then was out. I could still feel the effects of the shock treatments each time. It was horrible! I could taste the medicine from the injections afterward for several months. Not only did I experience this, but in my dreams I was going through the same treatments all over again. When I remember the severe treatments I endured, these were absolutely barbaric methods to rid me of the voices. The treatments never got rid of the voices, they were there after every treatment. They never left! I particularly remember after one treatment when I was told to get off the bed, make it up and start singing.

I learned how the voices would begin an argument especially with my husband, they would tell me what to say and how to answer him. He became angry as well as frustrated with me. We couldn't discuss any subject without both becoming angry and frustrated.

I thought to myself that I didn't want him to become so upset with me, yet I couldn't stop. I didn't understand how to stop the control of the voices, despite all the shock treatments that I was given. If I told him I was still hearing voices, he would put me back in the hospital for more. The thought of going back became a nightmare!

I became desperate over the situation and I decided I must leave and go to my mothers in Houston. I waited until he made a business trip out of town, found a baby sitter and then took my car and drove home to my mother. I didn't feel love and understanding from my husband and he certainly wouldn't accept my condition if I told him the truth. My mother was taking care of my youngest child when I was first hospitalized and he was still with her.

My husband returned home, finding me gone and the children with a baby sitter. He called my mother and found me there, saying very unkind things about me. He never understood my personal needs, nor the overwhelming job of taking care of the children. He left me with a tremendous amount of responsibility to shoulder alone. He was always wrapped up in himself and his job.

Chapter Eight

During the time I was at my mothers, I visited my namesake, an Aunt Betty. She had been a teacher in the public school system. I always respected and loved her and felt she might have some answers for me about my condition. I ask, "Do you believe there is a real devil?" "No" she said. I told her how my tongue couldn't speak words many times, that something was keeping me from talking. I felt I was being controlled and couldn't do what I wanted to do. I never took drugs, never drank alcohol, or smoked. She ignored what I said, then stated that she heard through the family I had received the baptism of the Holy Spirit and spoke in tongues. She thought it was absolutely wonderful!

According to her answers and our discussion,

I decided I couldn't trust what she had to say and decided something was very wrong because of my dreadful condition as the voices were unbearable. If I had the Holy Spirit, why did I have to go through such an ordeal with all the shock treatments, stay locked up in the hospital away from my children? It didn't ad up nor make any sense to me. I felt I would never overcome these demanding, controlling voices.

One afternoon while napping on my mother's sofa with my Bible beneath my pillow, I awoke. I pulled the Bible from under my pillow, and set it in my lap. The pages of the Bible opened. I looked down reading for the first time. I read 2 Timothy 1:7 "For God hath not given us the Spirit of Fear, but of Power, Love and a Sound Mind." I read it again and was shocked! I could hardly believe what I had read!! I read the same verse over and over again. I was stunned! No fear? Love? Sound Mind? It was such a revelation to me that I sat the rest of the day till night rehearsing the verse in my mind constantly- I was connecting all the painful ordeal of shock treatments and all the situations I had endured. For the first time since I heard the voices, I began questioning my experiences. I had been obeying what I thought was guidance and directions from the Holy

Spirit! I remember the first tongue speaking people that I met. They were so kind, saying such beautiful prayers, then would go off in tongues. They wanted me to read in the Book of Acts that I needed the baptism of the Holy spirit in order to be a true witness for Jesus. I was impressed by their sincerity. Just listening to them and observing their praying, I felt they must really be speaking to a Holy God. They said the tongues was a sign for unbelievers and was a gift from heaven for the believer. They acted as if it were a guaranteed passport to heaven.

I had seen others laying on the floor "slain in the Spirit" at some of the meetings I had attended. I was still in shock finding words in the Bible that held the key to my understanding. I knew I didn't have a sound mind, and I knew it, as the voices kept me in fear and obedience. Since God's word tells me that He gives me a sound mind, then if my experiences were not from the Holy Spirit, then where and what is it? I couldn't put my finger on it, but God's word began to fill my mind and I repeated the same verse over and over in my mind, "no fear, power, love and a sound mind." I went to bed that same night with God's words in my mind. During the middle of the night I felt the presence of something in my room. I heard loud laughing, Only I could hear. I heard a voice speak saying, "there is no real devil" and it kept laughing. I shouted, saying out loud, "there is a real devil!" The shout waked up my mother and sister. My sister said to my mother, "she's still crazy mother, she's still crazy!"

Little did my family realize the suffering I had been through. When I discovered the Word of God giving me the truth, I began to feel for the first time I had the answer.

My precious mother is deceased now, but I knew she had the entire church praying for me all those years.. She suffered greatly for my sake. After discovering these verses I wanted to go back home to my children., I knew I would face an angry husband, but I didn't care because the truth I found was more precious than anyone's hostility. Even though I found God's word of truth, I was till plagued by the voices and knew they would try to pit my husband and I against one another. I stayed continually on guard after arriving home. If my husband knew I still heard voices, it would be a return to the same treatments.

Chapter Nine

My husband was calm since I was back with the children. He never admitted the ordeal of my illness affected him, yet he was glad when I came home. His responsibility and care of the children during my absence made him more aware of how much he had depended on me. The housekeeper he had hired was dismissed now that I was back.

My husband had been responsible for my being hospitalized and enduring all the shock treatments. I was very angry at him. I felt he never really concerned himself about me personally, that I was only someone to take care of the children. I felt I was always on duty because he never concerned himself about my personal needs. I didn't feel loved by my husband as I was left alone to manage without his help. I became the mother figure that could handle any situation without his being around. I felt he was to blame for my condition.

I realized I would have to change my attitude towards him called "forgiveness." God's word was the change needed in my life. How could I have a "sound mind" if I ignored His word. I decided to turn to God for my comfort and love. I loved the Lord and knew I needed to change my attitude towards my husband in order to get well and honor God. How would I do this? I spent hours in prayer, talking with the Lord how to overcome these "hate" feelings. I told God that He would have to teach me how to love my husband again and forgive him. "You have to love him for me, because I can't do it!" I said to God. It would be very difficult, yet 1 was determined to make it work.

After the evening meals and the children were in bed asleep, I would take long walks away from the house. My husband never knew the real reason, only that I needed the exercise. Not only was I trying to overcome my hate and anger, but trying desperately to overcome the voices. I resisted not to speak what the voices would tell me to say to him as I knew it would lead to an argument. I refused to be drawn by their words. I would pray soon as I left out the front door. I walked block after block in the neighborhood praying out loud to God pouring out my hurts and strong feelings of resentments and all the wrongs against me. I knew I could never share my true feelings as my husband was the kind of person that never expressed his own feelings, so how could he understand mine? It became difficult to talk with him unless it was about his work. I couldn't appreciate anything about him at the time. It took a long time for me to accept him again in my heart.. He wasn't too happy about me either, as he had been inconvenienced during my absence.

I felt I was constantly in a battle to pursue my goal in becoming well. I was still battling against the voices repeating 2 Timothy 1:7 constantly, and at night would stay in prayer on my knees. I claimed that same verse continually, thinking the voices might leave. I knew I needed extra help learning I just couldn't continue doing this on my own.

I finally decided to join a Bible Study Group. I desperately needed help and felt if I knew God's word I could get rid of the voices. I never read the Bible before. I was only encouraged by those that spoke tongues to seek for the Holy Spirit The voices confused me at times...as I was needing the true Holy Spirit to lead and guide me. At one of the Bible studies I attended there was a young woman from India, a guest speaker. She gave her personal testimony about giving her life to Jesus after she tried to commit suicide. She stated that the knife she held to kill herself fell out of her hands as if something caused it She had been searching for answers in her life, going to different churches, but never finding answers, finally decided to end her life After her testimony, and the Bible study ended, I sought her for personal prayer, never explaining my reasons.

Chapter Ten

The following morning my phone rang and it was her. She ask did I sleep well last night I told her my sleep was very disturbing that I slept very little. She told me what happened when she prayed for me. She saw four demons leave my body. I was not sure, yet I had already experienced so much pain and suffering I knew she must be telling the truth. I had spent continuous nights on my knees praying to be released from the torment of my condition.

One day I was being so harassed I couldn't stop crying. There came a knock at my door. I opened it to find a middle age salesman. He saw me crying and ask what was wrong. When I told him, he told me straight out, "why lady, the devil is trying to destroy you! that's why your in this shape." The demons were still around to harass me. He had prayer with me and explained more of the Bible to me. I'm sure God must have sent him.

I started studying my Bible in the early morning hours while my children were asleep. Children take a lot of care and it was the only way I could find time to study. I began to hear less and less of the voices.

I longed to go home and be with my mother. I had grown weary mentally and emotionally needing a change. My husband came home one evening and announced the company was transferring him to Houston. Hearing the news, my joy was overwhelming! All I could do was praise the Lord! I knew without a doubt that my prayers had been answered. I felt for the first time in three years that my journey through hell was ending. I needed peace above all things. Jesus was my only source of strength during the trials I endured. I knew I needed to understand more about my condition and to be completely healed. I'm positive I was like the Gadarene demoniac that Jesus healed, possessed by demons. This story is found in .Luke 8:27-39.

Jesus' mission on this earth is to "set the captives free." (Luke 4:18) I definitely was a captive of Satan's and he would like to destroy not only me, but others he can deceive. He's an expert in deception and lies, and has been at it long before the world was created. The demons, known as fallen angels, knew exactly who Jesus was and still is, as these fallen angels are still in our world today although invisible. We cannot see into the invisible world as Jesus did. These same invisible beings continue their assaults and attacks creating pain and suffering on the human race. Not only was I being vexed by demon voices at night, I was being gouged in my ribs till the constant pain awoke me and I would call out to Jesus before it would stop. I was afraid to go back to sleep for fear it would start all over again. At times I was being choked and couldn't breathe. I would slide off my bed onto my knees and start praying.

These same evil fallen angels of Satan's cause millions of people to believe in the hereafter with their lies saying their dead loves ones are in heaven. They appear in forms that resemble their dead loved ones, even speaking like them, making one believe they are real. They will tell a loved one some unknown secret about their deceased husband or wife known only to them. This contributes to their erroneous belief that their loved one is in heaven. It becomes so real to them and they believe the lies.

God's word will clear up one's understanding about death. Death has always been a mystery. If it

weren't for Jesus and God's word, we would still believe like the pagans before Jesus came. Jesus death
and resurrection gives all believers hope. Samuel,
the Prophet had died. King Saul consulted a witch
at Endor to bring up the Prophet Samuel. God de-
clares that "these things are an abomination unto
the Lord." (Deuteronomy 18:12) God's word de-
clares in the book of Deuteronomy, chapter 19, verses 9,10,11,12 for his people not have anything to do
with an enchanter, a witch, charmer, or a consulter
with familiar spirits, or a wizard, or a necroman-
cer. The majority of people today believe when you
die you go straight to heaven. God's word tells the
truth, not based on lies or fables. His word teach-
es that the dead know not anything. "For the living know that they shall die: but the dead know not
anything." (Ecclesiastes 9:5) Besides healing people,
and casting out devils, like the Cananites' daughter that was grievously vexed with a devil; and was
made whole by her great faith in Jesus, Jesus raised
others from the dead. Jairus' daughter was raised
to life by Jesus. (Matthew 9:24) Mary and Martha's
brother Lazarus, died and was already buried and in
the grave, was brought back to life by Jesus, (St John
11:1-44.) Jesus told Martha, "I am the resurrection
and life." when questioned by Martha about her

brother's being resurrected. Jesus calls death a sleep. (St John 11:11) A person is unconscious not knowing time has passed.. When Lazarus was brought back to life he wasn't in heaven, neither were the others that were raised from the dead. Jesus didn't tell Lazarus to "come down" but to "come forth." Also, in Acts 2:29, the patriarch David, is both dead and buried, and his sepulcher is there today, awaiting the resurrection.

All this wondering why people hear voices, carry out orders given to them by the voices?" Its not some chemical imbalance in one's brain that causes this … its real!!

Chapter Eleven

We live at a time when unseen fallen angels are destroying and taking lives. Trouble in the world is increasing. God's heavenly holy angels are holding back the four winds of the earth. (Revelation 7:1). Sin is increasing. Hearts are failing for the things coming on the earth. Hearts are becoming harden to the voice of the Holy Spirit. The unpardonable sin is being developed. Treason against the Government of God is growing by leaps and bounds. Only a few are listening and heeding the Counsel of the True Witness (Revelation 3:14).

I wonder how many souls have sought for the healing of their own minds? And how long were they in a condition like my own, hearing voices, voices that tormented them? The media and daily newspapers tell stories of mothers that killed their own children because the voices or supposedly, God, spoke and told her to do it. The voices are so real, so demanding, so convincing, that one yields against their own will, and carries out the demands of the voices. Its happened many times, not just with mothers, but others that yielded their own will, being controlled, not able to resist. No one is able to understand why these people perform terrible acts that causes some one's death. It's a mystery to everyone, yet many blame these acts on the use of drugs, or some disease of the mind, or someone that has a chemical imbalance in their brain. A well known mother living in Houston, took the life of her five children. She was found insane. What made her do it? She wasn't in her right mind. Could it have been all the lies she believed regarding the salvation of her children. An unseen power had control of her mind to carry out such a plan. When a person is demon possessed, they are not their own. They do the bidding of the demon.

The greatest physicians or scientists do not understand that invisible forces control an individual to carry out commands given to them. A physician will take an x-ray or an MR I (magnetic reasoning images) of the brain, before and after, looking for the answer, then medicate the patient with a drug or shock treatment* There is a record of history revealed of terrible inhuman treatments given to patients that have suffered from delusions. The treatments can totally remove a person from reality, loosing all their memories. A shock treatment is like receiving electricity to the brain. Parts of the brain are deadened.

The brain is under a deadly assault by more than just the unseen. Marketing lethal drugs, while concealing the results of studies that reveal deadly side effects, should be a legal offense. The drug scene has captured Americans, especially the youth. The brain is being attacked in today's society by unseen forces. All ages are being attacked and subjected to poisonous chemicals found in the atmosphere, in the foods and in the water that effects the brain. The public is beginning to suspect that the foods they are eating causes cancers. Cancer is like a plague. Ask how someone passed away? The answer is always, someone had cancer. Cancer treatment centers are springing up even in smaller communities like those in major cities. The treatments wipe out one's immune system effecting the good blood cells as well as the cancerous cells. It doesn't take shock treatments to assault the human brain, its being done chemically through the foods. Aspartame, chemically produced, is considered a safe product to use, however, studies indicate that it isn't. Aspartame is found in diet drinks damaging to one's health. Another product that is questionable is, monosodium glutamate (msg), a chemical preservative that effects one's appetite. It is a flavor enhancer to increase one's intake of food. No wonder Americans are overweight! Remember, the fat you eat is the fat you wear! And MSG is included in almost every product on the grocery shelf. It is important to read labels of all products and discover the added chemicals to avoid. Chemicals added to foods is a sure way of destroying the brain.

I would question all foods that one buys to see how it will effect ones' health as our nation has entered into a global marketing and foods once grown only in the U.S. are coming in from countries all over the world. The public has become more aware of the foods they consume and to avoid questionable meats, have become vegetarians or vegans. A vegetarian is someone who lives on a diet of grains, beans, lentils, nuts, seeds, fresh vegetables and fruits with or without the use of dairy products and eggs. A vegetarian does not eat any meat, poultry, fish, shellfish or crustacean, or slaughter-by-products such as gelatin or animal fats. Many vegetarians choose a plant based diet because of the unwanted fat found in animals and dairy products. Some folks experience better health by substituting flesh foods for foods from soy products found in today's grocery markets. The Chinese have lived on soy products for years. According to a recent article found in a noted magazine, obesity in China is very rare.

I found a book, called "Ministry of Healing" authored by E.G. White, and read a chapter on "Mind Cure." She states, "the relationship that exists between the mind and the body is very intimate. When one is affected, the other sympathizes. The condition of the mind affects the health to a far greater degree than many realize and many of the diseases from which men suffer are the result of mental depression. Grief, anxiety, discontent, remorse, guilt, distrust, all tend to break down the life forces, and to invite decay and death. Further into the reading I learned that courage, hope, faith, sympathy, and love promotes health and prolongs life. "A contented mind, a cheerful spirit, is health to the body and strength too the soul." "A Merry heart doeth good like a medicine" is the prescription given by the author of the Bible. I came across a statement in regards to "mind control." This had nothing to do with hearing voices. As stated from the same book, it is not God's purpose that any human being should yield his mind and will to the control of another, becoming passive instrument in his hands. No one is to merge his individuality in that of another. He is not to look to another human being as the source of healing. His dependence must be in God alone. Before I learned the truth in God's word, my mind and speech was being controlled.

Many times I wanted to speak or say something, but couldn't. It was like there was something preventing me from speaking. When I tried to carry out my own will to do something, I couldn't. A stronger power controlled me, to do the things I knew in my own mind that I shouldn't do. There was a personal daily struggle to overcome the voices. I was crying for relief on the inside, never sharing my torment»

I attended a funeral of a deceased relative one day. When it was my turn to pass by and look at the deceased, I instantly wished I could exchange places., My misery was unexplainable to anyone. My only refuge was my faith in God seeking his help.

Chapter 12
Depression

I don't claim to know all the answers for people who suffer from this. I do know my own experience and learned how our enemy, the Devil, assaults human beings through depression, so they can't rise above their feelings of despair. He disguises himself cleverly because truth would stop him. One day I found myself weeping uncontrollably. I couldn't stop. While I was crying I received a phone call from my pastor. He said he felt impressed to call me, then ask if there was anything wrong. He suggested we pray. As soon as prayer was sought, I stopped crying. Whatever was creating my depression at the time, suddenly left. It was gone! I'll never forget the experience. Its been my experience that prayer to

God works. He hears and answers a personal prayer according to the circumstance. It's a matter of one's faith. He wants us to come to Him at any time, and for anything that we can't handle. He's the power in control, not our enemy. God seeks only good for us and our happiness.

He's mankind's answer to their problems on this earth. No other name under heaven has the authority to do this. God's son, Jesus Christ fought against the enemy and won the battle for our souls. He releases us from Satan's domain and gives us freedom. He saves us from our sins, offering each person, a brand new start in life. We all have a second chance to live. When one is baptized and believes that Jesus saves them from their sins, they are allied to a heavenly kingdom and become sons and daughters of the Living God. They have found God is their real father and creator, and they belong to a large family.

In the Bible's written word, terms such as emotional stress, challenging situations, resolving situations, self-destructive behavior, depression, are never expressed, yet the human race is marked by stressful daily experiences, common to all. Depression is a very well known factor afflicting the majority of people.

There are some well written books dealing with

depression having to do with one's own physical health. Sometimes depression can be early signs of nutritional depletion physically. The individual cannot continue with poor health and expect to feel good. One needs to investigate what their body needs. Fresh Fruits and vegetables are necessary to sustain good health, nutritionally speaking as well as sustaining good mental and emotional health.

Whatever a person eats or drinks can and will effect one's mind and thinking. According to the Bible, God promises "peace" to disturbed minds as found in the book of Isaiah 26:3 "Thou wilt keep him in perfect peace, whose mind is stayed on thee: because he trusteth in thee." God's word is powerful. Hebrews 4:12, "For the word of God is quick, and powerful, and sharper than any two-edged sword, piercing even to the dividing asunder of soul and spirit, and of the joints and marrow, and is a discerner of the thoughts and intents of the heart." God's word has the answer to one's ills especially effecting their minds.

My mind was anything but well until I found the words in the Bible how God gives us a sound mind. I fought daily the battle against forces that tried to conquer me. Once I learned the truth in God's word, I fought diligently to become sane with His help. I was young with three children to raise when all of this happened to me, yet, even at my older age now, it's an experience that guards me against the forces of evil and my total allegiance is to Jesus that saved me. I owe Him my very life, and wouldn't want to be without Him. My testimony is to help those who are struggling and battling against unseen forces of Satan's evil angels. God's word has healing powers. To stay mentally and morally well one must recognize that Jesus, who is the Author and Finisher of our faith, is the answer. He will protect one from the onslaughts of Satan, and heavenly angels of the Lord will keep diligent watch-care over you, as God knows each one personally.

God bless all those who look to Jesus for their safety. He bestows his great love, compassion and care upon each individual in this present world regardless of their race or color, because he created them all. Look to Jesus as He is bigger than all your problems.

We invite you to view the complete
selection of titles we publish at:

www.ASPECTBooks.com

Scan with your mobile
device to go directly
to our website.

Please write or email us your praises, reactions,
or thoughts about this or any other book we publish at:

AB ASPECT Books
www.ASPECTBooks.com

P.O. Box 954
Ringgold, GA 30736

info@ASPECTBooks.com

TEACH Services, Inc., titles may be purchased in bulk for
educational, business, fund-raising, or sales promotional use.
For information, please e-mail:

BulkSales@ASPECTBooks.com

Finally, if you are interested in seeing
your own book in print, please contact us at

publishing@ASPECTBooks.com

We would be happy to review your manuscript for free.